CAMBRIDGE INTRODUCTION TO WORLD HISTORY
GENERAL EDITOR · TREVOR CAIRNS

Life in a medieval monastery

DURHAM PRIORY IN THE FIFTEENTH CENTURY

Anne Boyd

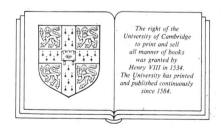

The right of the
University of Cambridge
to print and sell
all manner of books
was granted by
Henry VIII in 1534.
The University has printed
and published continuously
since 1584.

CAMBRIDGE UNIVERSITY PRESS
Cambridge
New York New Rochelle
Melbourne Sydney

Drawings by Ann Mieke
Maps by Reg Piggott

Published by the Press Syndicate of the University of Cambridge
The Pitt Building, Trumpington Street, Cambridge CB2 1RP
32 East 57th Street, New York, NY 10022, USA
10 Stamford Road, Oakleigh, Melbourne 3166, Australia

© Cambridge University Press 1975, 1987

Library of Congress Catalogue Card Number: 74-14438

ISBN 0 521 33724 0
(*The Monks of Durham* ISBN 0 521 20647 2)

First published as *The Monks of Durham* 1975
Reprinted 1977, 1984
Reissued as *Life in a Medieval Monastery* 1987
Reprinted 1987, 1989

Printed photolitho in Great Britain by
Ebenezer Baylis & Son Ltd, The Trinity Press,
Worcester, and London

Acknowledgements

The author and publisher wish to thank the following for permission
to reproduce illustrations:
front cover, pp. 8, 15, 18, 26, 27 (Lindisfarne Gospels), 36, 40 the
British Library Board; back cover, pp. 6, 9, 11, 17, 19, 21, 23, 25, 28,
37, 39, 46, 47, 48, the Dean and Chapter, Durham Cathedral; pp.5, 31,
32, 38 Committee for Aerial Photography, Cambridge University; p. 10
Walter Scott, Bradford; pp. 17 (clock), 19 (cloister), 23 (vault), 29, 40
(triforium), 45 Cambridge University Library; p. 27 the Master and
Fellows of Corpus Christi College, Cambridge; p. 44 Library of the
Escorial, Madrid.
The author and publisher would also like to thank Dr Barrie Dobson,
Reader in History at the University of York, for his help in the prepara-
tion of this book. Much of the information about the Durham monks
is derived from his *Durham Priory, 1400–1450*, published by Cambridge
University Press in 1973. Thanks are also due to the staffs of the
Chapter Library, Durham and of the muniments room of the Depart-
ment of Paleography and Diplomatic, Durham University, for their
help and co-operation.

front cover: *St. Cuthbert and his monks. The picture is
from a twelfth-century manuscript formerly in Durham
priory and now in the British Library. The MS is Bede's
Life of St Cuthbert.*

back cover: *The burial of a prior. From a fifteenth-
century obit roll at Durham (see page 46).*

Contents

There never was such a thing as a standard medieval monastery. Some were big and rich, some small and poor. Some were in towns, others in the countryside, some in remote isolation. There were different orders with different rules. As times changed, life inside the monasteries changed too.

From the evidence which remains today the historian can give a picture of life in a monastery. This book describes a great monastery at Durham, in the north of England, towards the end of the Middle Ages. It has been chosen because more is known about Durham priory than about other monasteries in England at that time. The book may also help to answer some of the questions many people ask about monastic life: what are monks trying to do? Is it worth doing? How does it affect other people? Did the monks of Durham succeed? Why did it all end so suddenly?

1   The shrine of St Cuthbert

England in the 8th century

The story of St Cuthbert

In the tenth century the small wooden church at Chester-le-Street held what many people thought to be the most precious treasure in all England – the body of St Cuthbert. Pilgrims made long journeys to pray at the shrine of the saint and to ask his help. What was there about Cuthbert that led the English to look to him for protection in times of trouble? He had lived some 300 years earlier, and had spent most of his life as a simple monk.

Cuthbert was born about A.D. 635, probably in Northumbria. According to later (but misleading) legend, his parents were of Irish origin with royal connections. As the story goes, the boy Cuthbert – like St Patrick earlier in Ireland – was guarding a flock of sheep in the hills when he had a vision or dream. He seemed to see the soul of a holy man being carried to heaven by angels. Next day he heard that Bishop Aidan had died. Aidan was a monk from the Celtic monastery at Iona who had come to convert the Northumbrians to Christianity. He was made bishop of Lindisfarne, a little island off the coast, and founded a monastery there. Cuthbert was so impressed by the dream that he decided to become a monk too. He went to Melrose, another monastery founded by the Irish monks.

There are plenty of stories of Cuthbert's life as a monk – of his holiness in the monastery, his energy in preaching to the people, his care in obeying the rule of the monks, even of the miracles he did. Later he was sent to another monastery, at Ripon, and then to Lindisfarne. Eventually he became prior there. (The prior was the monk who, in the abbot's absence, had charge of the other monks.) But Cuthbert always thought he could please God best by spending his time alone in prayer. He went to live all by himself on one of the Farnes, tiny islands further out to sea. There he made a little cell, or hut, in the rocks just as the Irish monks used to do on islands off the Irish coast.

The Inner Farne Islands, looking north-west. St Cuthbert lived as a hermit on one of these islands off the coast of Northumberland about 6 miles (10km) south-east of Lindisfarne.

The other monks came to see him from time to time and brought food until he found out how to catch enough fish for himself and grow some grain. Yet Cuthbert was not allowed to spend the rest of his life on Farne for, in 685, he was made bishop of Lindisfarne. For two years he visited the churches of his diocese and preached to the people again. Then he felt that his life was ending so he resigned from being bishop and went back to Farne where he died in 687.

Cuthbert was buried in the church at Lindisfarne. Soon many people came to pray at his tomb. Eleven years later the monks decided to move his body to a more important part of the church. When they opened the coffin they found that the body had not decayed but was still 'more like a sleeping than a dead man'. This was taken as a further proof of his great holiness. The monks were to need this proof in the difficult years of strife that followed. Though the kingdoms of the north changed hands, and were torn by feuds, Cuthbert was honoured and appealed to by all until he became the most famous saint in the whole of the north of England.

In 793 Vikings attacked the island of Lindisfarne itself. The monastery recovered from this single raid but by 875 the situation was so dangerous that the bishop, Eardwulf, decided to move the body of Cuthbert to a less exposed place. The bishop, with the abbot Eadred and a company of monks, travelled about for seven years looking for a home. Eventually they settled at Chester-le-Street. For a hundred years there was peace. Once again pilgrims travelled to the shrine of the saint.

5

Fragments of the oak coffin made for the body of St Cuthbert in 698. Carvings of the Virgin Mary and the Apostles can be seen on the sides. The photograph shows an attempt to reconstruct the coffin.

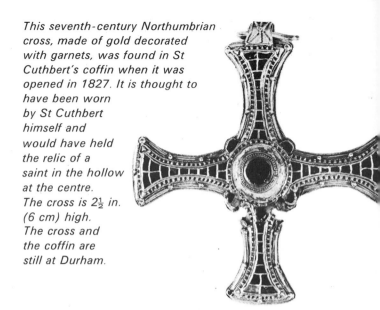

This seventh-century Northumbrian cross, made of gold decorated with garnets, was found in St Cuthbert's coffin when it was opened in 1827. It is thought to have been worn by St Cuthbert himself and would have held the relic of a saint in the hollow at the centre. The cross is 2½ in. (6 cm) high. The cross and the coffin are still at Durham.

Cuthbert comes to Durham

It is not certain why Aldhun, the bishop in 995, decided to move again. Probably he feared a renewal of Viking attacks and hoped to find a safer place. He travelled south, taking the body of Cuthbert first to the abbey of Ripon and then to a place on the River Wear where, so the legend says, Cuthbert's coffin refused to budge, and thus made it known that the saint wished to stop. The travellers found themselves on a high rocky promontory of land surrounded on three sides by the river – ideal protection for the shrine of their saint. Ideal also for Bishop Aldhun's son-in-law, Uhtred (the future earl of Northumberland) who needed a strong fortification against Vikings, Scots and rivals. It may not have been Cuthbert alone who chose the place.

Aldhun saw to the building of the first stone church at what is now called Durham. Around it 'St Cuthbert's folk' lived in small houses, hardly more than huts. This was no longer an organised monastery such as had been centuries ago on Lindisfarne. Some of the priests had married. Many monastic customs had been lost in the years of trouble and disturbance though the devotion to St Cuthbert remained strong and people still came on pilgrimage.

The land on the promontory was cleared and levelled.

More houses were built. Masons who had come to build the church stayed to enjoy the protection of the saint. It seems likely that some fortifications were built at this time for in 1006, and again in 1040, the Scots attacked Durham. The town continued to grow as houses spread along the promontory and on the top of the hills across the river.

In 1066 England was invaded by William, Duke of Normandy, who soon established his followers to rule in all the important areas of England. To Durham he sent Robert Comyn to subdue the town. He treated the inhabitants so brutally that, as the Normans were celebrating their victory they were surprised and massacred by rebels. As a result King William came himself and saw to the re-fortifying of the town. In 1072 he ordered a castle to be built on land to the north of the church and commanded that a curfew bell should be rung at 9 p.m. All the townsfolk had to stay indoors at night and put out lights and fires. A bell is still rung in Durham at 9 p.m. but the rule about putting out lights has not lasted so long!

A year earlier, in 1071, a Norman, Walcher, had been appointed bishop. When at Durham he lived in the castle for protection from the people who were still hostile. Because he wanted to learn more about the people he had to govern he began to read about their history, especially in the writings

A bird's-eye view of the River Wear at Durham as it may have been before the monks settled there.

A stone carving high on an outside wall of Durham cathedral recalls the legend of the coming of St Cuthbert. The saint wanted his coffin to rest at 'Dunholme'. But where was this? Then a woman was heard calling, 'Where is my cow?' 'At Dunholme', another replied. The procession followed the woman until the cow, and Dunholme, were found. The present carving replaced an earlier one in about 1775. ▷

of Bede. Bede was a monk of Jarrow who, about A.D. 730, had written a famous life of St Cuthbert and an even more famous history of the English Church. About 1050, a priest at Durham, Aelfred, son of Westow, boldly removed the bones of Bede from the ruined abbey at Jarrow and carried them to Durham where they were honoured along with St Cuthbert's.

When Bishop Walcher read the story of Cuthbert he began to think about having a real monastery at Durham, just as there had been centuries ago at Lindisfarne. To understand

7

why he wanted monks, a group of men living a settled well-organized and peaceful life, it is necessary to know something about St Benedict, the great founder of the Benedictine, or Black Monks, as his followers were called.

St Benedict

Benedict was the son of a well-to-do family. He was born in central Italy about A.D. 480, at a time when Italy was being overrun by barbarians. There was no longer an emperor in Rome. The armies of the eastern emperor in Byzantium were scarcely able to protect the cities and the civilization that the Romans had built.

Benedict had the idea – as Cuthbert was later to have – of going off by himself to pray. He did not want to be involved in the struggle for power, the greed and ambition and selfishness that rich men and rulers fell into. He wanted more time to think about God, and about the life of Jesus Christ, and to try to be a better Christian. For a while he lived alone in a cave near Subiaco. Then other men came to join him. They asked him to teach them to live as monks.

In order to guide them, Benedict set out in his 'little rule for beginners' the main things a Christian ought to do 'if he truly seeks God'. He should live in peace with others, not always wanting his own way, or having an exaggerated idea of himself. He should live simply, not wanting to own many things in order to feel important and secure. He should pray often, and read the Bible.

Because a group of people who are trying to live together peacefully need to agree about how to do things, Benedict also wrote down many details: how the monastery was to be governed, what the special duties were, what prayers should be said and when, what kind of a man the abbot ought to be, how guests should be cared for, and so on. Every monk had to promise to obey the abbot, and to stay in the abbey all his life. Although a monk promised not to marry, life in the monastery should be like a family with the abbot as father. The abbot was elected for life by the monks. All the needs of the monks were to be provided within the monastery. Men came there from different ranks of society: the sons of peasants who could neither read nor write, as well as the children of noble families who had been educated in the monastery school. But all were to live together in peace and order.

8

St Benedict gives the Rule to his monks. A picture from an eleventh-century manuscript. Many medieval books were hand-written by monks, especially in the early Middle Ages. The examples on the following pages show how the handwriting changed over the years.

Benedict's ideas were especially important in a world where organized government and trade and communications were breaking down under the barbarian invasions. His monasteries were self-contained 'islands', able to survive for long periods without support from governments and towns.

About 525 he moved from Subiaco to Monte Cassino where

he founded another monastery. (There is still a monastery there today, although the buildings have been destroyed and rebuilt over the centuries.) He died about 550 leaving a Rule that gradually came to be obeyed by communities of monks all over Western Europe.

Towards the end of the sixth century a Benedictine monk became pope. He is known as Gregory the Great because he did so much for the Church. One thing he did was to send a band of monks to England. It was this mission, in 596–7, which began the conversion of the English to Christianity and its leader, Augustine, became the first archbishop of Canterbury.

Over the centuries, the style of life in the great monasteries of France and England had changed from that of St Benedict's day. The buildings became more splendid, the prayers more elaborate. The monks worked less in the fields and spent more time in study and the writing and decorating of beautiful books. The English monasteries had some characteristics of their own. The buildings were altered to suit the colder English climate and included a special room with a fire for warmth in winter. The English monasteries were not as cut off from the life of the country as Benedict had intended his monks to be. Kings and queens became their patrons or guardians. The monastery church might also be the cathedral church of a large region and the bishop would live with the monks. The abbey bells were rung on Sundays and feast days for the people to come to church, and on special occasions monks and people would hold processions through the town.

In the library at Durham cathedral is a copy of St Augustine's Commentary on the Psalms, probably made about 1088. This initial shows Bishop William of St Calais wearing the robes of a priest and with his head shaven in a monk's crown or 'tonsure'. Above is the picture of Christ and kneeling at his feet is the black-robed monk, Benjamin, who made the picture.

The Black Monks at Durham

The monks of the English abbeys, for all their connections with the great abbeys on the Continent, thus felt themselves to be a part of the English Church. They read the history of Christianity in England and especially the lives of the great English saints. It is therefore not so surprising that, just at the time when the Norman, Bishop Walcher, was thinking of how he could bring monks to Durham, three monks set out from the great abbey of Evesham in the valley of the Severn to visit the northern shrines. They wanted to see the remains of the great monasteries that Bede had written about. They went first to Jarrow where, filled with enthusiasm for the austerities of Cuthbert and the early monks, they made themselves a simple place to live among the ruins. The three,

Aldwin, Reinfrid and Aelfwig, were helped by the people who lived round about. More monks came from the south to join them. Bishop Walcher was interested and wanted to help them too, but, in 1080, he was murdered.

The next bishop of Durham, William, had himself been a monk at a famous abbey in France, St Calais. He, too, read about Cuthbert, and the old monks at Lindisfarne and Jarrow, and heard about Bishop Walcher's hopes. Before he had been in Durham a year he began discussions with King William, with Lanfranc, the archbishop of Canterbury, and with the pope. The result of all this was that in 1083 he brought all twenty-three monks from the new communities at Jarrow and Wearmouth to Durham, to make their vows at the shrine of St Cuthbert. Aldwin became the first prior.

The bishop himself was to be abbot of the new monastery

The nave of Durham cathedral looking eastwards towards the high altar. The great stone pillars and round arches of the twelfth-century church still stand. This was the first cathedral in England to have a roof completely vaulted in stone. In the later Middle Ages women were forbidden to cross the row of stones at the front of the picture.

but as he would have to look after the affairs of his diocese, and sometimes also those of the king, he would not have time to think about the day-to-day running of the monastery. The monk really in charge would be the prior. In most monasteries the prior was second-in-command to the abbot but because at Durham the prior ruled, the monastery was called a priory not an abbey.

Although the bishops of Durham were to have their differences with the monks, the bishop was after all the successor of St Cuthbert. It was right that he should be a powerful figure in the land. The monks were proud of his prestige. They were also to be grateful for his gifts.

Building the cathedral

The bishop gave the monks some land and soon began to plan the building of a great new church. Prior Aldwin died, but the next prior, Turgot, worked with the bishop on the building which was begun in 1093. By 1104 the building was ready for the body of St Cuthbert to be placed in the apse behind the high altar (see the plan on page 13).

In the splendid setting of the new cathedral the shrine grew in fame over the years until it could compare with that of St Edmund at Bury St Edmunds, and St Etheldreda at Ely – even, so the monks said, with that of the Apostle James at Compostella in Spain.

As St Cuthbert's fame grew other churches all over England were dedicated to him. Cuthbert became a very popular name for ships in the north-eastern ports. To St Cuthbert the monks attributed the victory at Neville's Cross, just outside Durham, against the Scots in 1346 when the Scottish King David was captured, while the monks, with St Cuthbert's banner, watched from a nearby hill. The signal of the victory was sent back to the cathedral where a hymn of thanks was sung from the central church tower.

An account, written late in the sixteenth century, describes the shrine of St Cuthbert as it was when crowds of pilgrims visited it around 1500. It tells of the shrine behind the high altar

> 'exalted with most curious workmanship of fine and costly green marble all limned and gilded with gold, having four seats or places convenient under the shrine for the pilgrims or lame men sitting on their knees to lean and rest on, in time of their devout offerings and fervent prayers to God and holy St Cuthbert for his miraculous relief and succour which, never being wanting, made the shrine to be so richly invested that it was estimated to be one of the most sumptuous monuments in all England; so great were the offerings and jewels that were bestowed upon it, and no less the miracles that were done by it, even in these latter days. . .'

The greatest ceremonies were on the feast day of St Cuthbert (20 March). On this day the wooden cover of the shrine was drawn up by means of a pulley in the vaulted roof and four

The twelfth-century bronze knocker on the north door of Durham cathedral. In a room above the door two servants were always on duty ready to open to anyone who knocked asking for 'sanctuary'. Anyone in danger of capture, even criminals, would be offered St Cuthbert's protection and no pursuer would dare to break this custom.

cords attached to the corners of the lid. As the rope was pulled a chime of six silver bells rang out, giving warning to all in the cathedral that the shrine was open and the coffin of the saint, with all its splendid decoration, could be seen. Nearby were cupboards or 'almerys' 'finely painted and gilded finely over with little images, very seemly and beautiful to behold'. In the almerys were the gifts and jewels brought by kings and nobles to honour St Cuthbert. The monks were especially proud of royal visitors. King Henry VI came in 1448, Richard III in 1483, and Margaret Tudor in 1503.

The pilgrims did not give only jewels for the shrine. Over the centuries land and money were given to the monks until Durham cathedral priory was the richest religious house north of York.

What kind of men were the Durham monks that people should hold them in such high regard? And how did they live? To understand the daily life of the monks we can look first at the buildings. A monastery is purpose-built.

The monastery buildings

The land encircled by the River Wear was divided into two by the cathedral which stood east–west across most of the peninsula. To the north was the bishop's castle, to the south the priory. As the number of monks increased the buildings had been extended and in 1416 there were forty monks living in a splendid group of buildings protected by the river.

The buildings surrounded a central court or cloister garth. On the north side was the nave of the cathedral, to the west the long first-floor dormitory with storerooms and 'warming room' below. On the south side was the dining hall, or refectory, with more storerooms below. Beyond these was the kitchen. In the south-east corner were the prior's apartments, while on the east side of the cloister were the chapter house, the parlour, and the library which was built beside the south transept of the cathedral. All around the inside of the cloister were four covered ways, or alleys, which had, on the north and west sides, little cubicles, or carrells, where the monks could read and write.

Further to the south of the main group of buildings was a greater courtyard surrounded by workshops, storerooms, stables and servants' quarters. To the south-west was the infirmary, the house where the sick and old received special care. To the east was the great gate on to the street which led down to the town.

Compare the plan opposite with the drawing made in the 1590s and the aerial photograph on page 38.

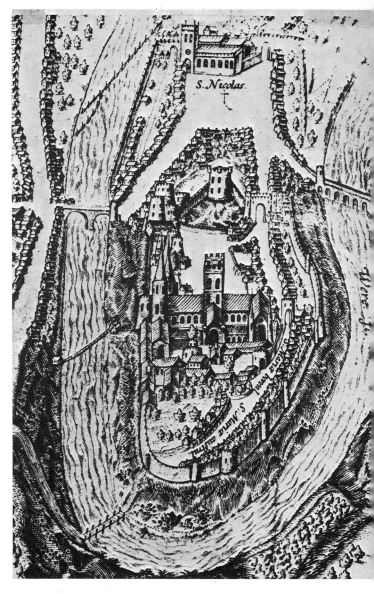

A bird's-eye view drawing of Durham made in the 1590s, about 150 years later than the period this book describes. In the fifteenth century there would probably have been fewer houses in the town but not much else would have been different.

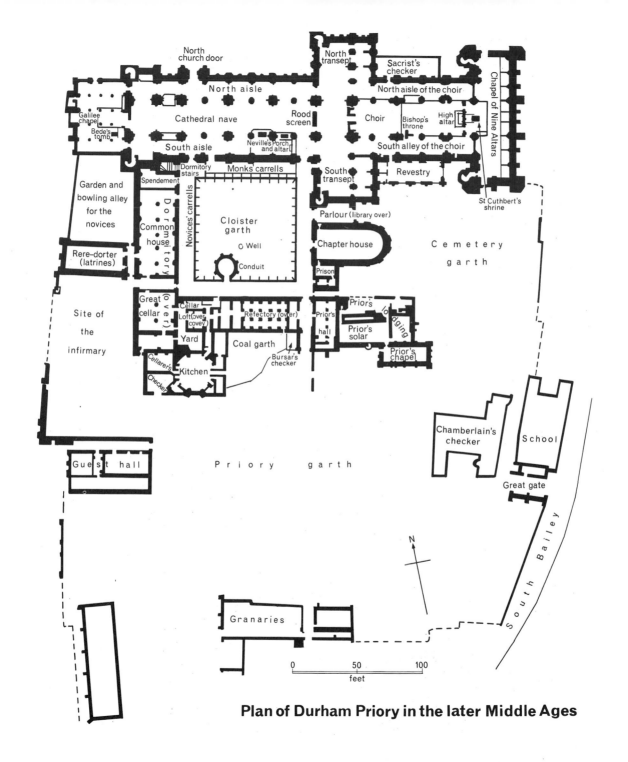

Plan of Durham Priory in the later Middle Ages

North church door

North transept

Sacrist's checker

Chapel of Nine Altars

North aisle

North aisle of the choir

Galilee chapel

Bede's tomb

Cathedral nave

Rood screen

Choir

Bishop's throne

High altar

South aisle

Neville's Porch and altar

South alley of the choir

Dormitory stairs

Monks' carrells

Spendement

South transept

Revestry

St Cuthbert's shrine

Garden and bowling alley for the novices

Novices' carrells

Cloister garth

Parlour (library over)

Cemetery garth

Common house

Dormitory

O Well

Conduit

Chapter house

Rere-dorter (latrines)

Prison

Site of the infirmary

Great cellar (over)

Cellar

Loft (over covey)

Refectory (over)

Priors lodging

Prior's hall

Prior's solar

Prior's chapel

Yard

Coal garth

Bursar's checker

Cellarer's Checker

Kitchen

Guest hall

Priory garth

Chamberlain's checker

School

Great gate

N

South Bailey

Granaries

0   50   100
feet

13

2 The daily life of the monks

In 1414 six young men asked to become monks at Durham priory. (We know some of their names: William Crayk, John Lumley and John Mody.) They were probably all in their late teens and may have been waiting for some time for the prior to name the day when they would be allowed to come. A prospective monk did not just turn up and expect to be admitted on the spot.

There were several reasons why the young men had to wait. St Benedict says in his Rule 'To him that newly comes to conversion, let not an easy entrance be granted. . .' 'Try the spirits, if they be of God.' In other words, give the young man time to think about it. Also, it was important not to take more monks than the priory could afford to keep. Although the monks were thought to be wealthy, they often had difficulty in making ends meet. As their income was enough to support about forty monks it was best to keep to this number. So when a few of the old monks had died, a few new ones could be allowed to join. Also it was easier to train several 'novices' together (as the new monks were called), and they might enjoy each other's company.

What the monks wore

At last the day was fixed. The young men arrived and spent a few days in the priory guest house preparing for the ceremony of receiving the monk's robes. This ceremony took place in the church. All the monks were present to welcome the newcomers. The prior gave each one a tunic, a black scapular and a cowl.

All the outer garments were made of a fairly heavy black woollen material. The drawings show how they were worn. Special prayers were said asking for help for the young men in 'truly seeking God' and in following the Rule of St Benedict. After the ceremony the new monks went to the novices' quarters. Each one was issued with the rest of his outfit, a change of undershirt, drawers, and tunic, and:

2 head caps	several pairs of white socks
2 pairs of slippers	a knife
2 pairs of boots	a belt, probably leather
an extra cowl	handkerchiefs
1 pair of gaiters	needles
2 pairs of blankets	writing materials

A modern artist's idea of the clothes the monks wore. The monk on the right is wearing a tunic and 'scapular'. The one on the left wears his cowl, the outer garment for all public occasions. Historians are not certain about exactly how the habit was made and you will see different versions in some of the medieval pictures in this book.

Where the monks came from

The newcomers must have wondered when they would ever get to know all the older monks who were to be their companions for the rest of their lives. For one thing all the monks dressed alike. For another, they were nearly all called either John, William, Thomas, Robert, Richard or Henry. This meant, of course, that most had second names. These second names give us a clue to where the monks came from. There were Durham family names (like the Raketts, Rihalls or Bonours), or names giving occupation or home town. It is clear from the lists of monks, still in the archives at Durham, that many came from the north-east of England and that many were from the middle ranks of society: sons of clerks and notaries and shopkeepers in Durham, of tenant farmers of the priory, of merchants of Hull or Newcastle.

Anyone of illegitimate birth, or anyone accused of being a 'bondman' and not free, could not become a monk of Durham priory.

We do not know anything about the families of William Crayk, John Lumley or John Mody but the priory records tell us something of other young men who joined the community about the same time.

It was the earl of Northumberland who, in 1441, suggested Richard Bell to the monks and asked Prior Wessington to keep an eye on him. Later, in 1443, the earl asked the prior to send Brother Thomas Holme to Durham College, Oxford. It was more usual for young men to be recommended by the monks themselves. The young monk, William Birden, was a relative of Richard Barton, the prior of the Durham house at Stamford. The warden of Durham College, Oxford sent young John Fishburn to Durham requesting that he should be accepted as a monk because 'he could sing well and wanted to be a monk'.

Boys who had served the monks' Masses in the cathedral, or who had been in the priory school, or the cathedral song school, might want to join the community. They would be well known to the monks who would need little advice from anyone else about whether to accept them.

After the clothing ceremony the novices slept in their own part of the dormitory. They attended the church services with the others. Each novice was given into the charge of an older monk who would teach him how things were done. The novice had to learn where his own place was in the church, the dormitory, the refectory and the chapter house. He also had to learn when to stand and sit during the long services in the church, how to serve at meals or to read aloud to the others if it was his turn.

He had to learn what to do at every hour of the day. Life in a monastery followed a strict timetable.

A drawing in a thirteenth-century French manuscript shows a young man joining a religious community by putting on his monastic habit. The bishop stands on the left while a senior monk, probably the abbot, helps to clothe him. The devil shown sitting on his shoulder will be driven away when he puts on the cowl.

A day in the life of a monk

The monks' day began at midnight – or as near to midnight as could be calculated by their clock, still a fairly new invention and liable to break down. Most of the monks slept in the great dormitory. This had been rebuilt just after 1400 as a long hall with a timbered roof: wooden screens were built to provide a cubicle for each monk. Two rows of windows lit the building. Those above were widely spaced tall windows; lower down, pairs of small windows set deep in the wall provided alcoves where the monks could read. The beds were probably the box beds usual at that time: a framework of boards with a criss-cross of rope that would hold a straw paillasse. There was probably straw on the floor too for warmth and some of the monks may have hung lengths of cloth on the walls to keep out the draughts.

The Rule of St Benedict says, 'Let them sleep each one in a separate bed, receiving bedding suitable to their manner of life, as the Abbot shall appoint.' They were supposed to sleep in one room, with a senior monk, or dean, to keep an eye on every ten monks. A candle should be kept burning all night. The rule instructed the deans to go the rounds several times during the night to see that all was in order. (It seems unlikely that this was done strictly – the deans would never get any sleep themselves.)

The monks were to 'sleep clothed and girded with belts or cords – but not with knives at their sides, lest perchance they wound themselves in their sleep'. They kept some clothes on in bed, partly because they had to be ready to go down quickly to Matins at midnight; also, at that time only wealthy people had special clothes for night wear.

Near the dormitory in a building known as the 'rere-dorter' were the latrines. Monastic builders usually paid careful attention to sanitation. It was usual to build a monastery near a stream and arrange the buildings so that the kitchens were higher up the stream and the latrines were built where the

Summer timetable	
Midnight	*Matins* in the church (about 1 hour) Then back to bed
6 a.m.	*Prime* in the church (about ½ hour) Breakfast Work or reading
9 a.m.	Chapter Mass in the church
10 a.m.	Chapter meeting in the chapter house
11 a.m.	High Mass in the church
12 noon	Dinner Then siesta
2 p.m.	*Nones* in the church (about ½ hour) Work
4 p.m.	Vespers in the church (about ½ hour) Work
6 p.m.	Supper
7 p.m.	*Compline*, the evening prayer, in the church (about ½ hour) Then to bed, later in summer than in winter

In winter Matins was a few hours later, and other adjustments were made throughout the day.

An artist's impression of a monastic dormitory. The dormitory at Durham is the best preserved in England and still has its original timber roof of 1400-4 (see photograph opposite): the room is now used as a cathedral museum and library.

stream flowed away from the monastery. In Durham there would be special problems about the water supply because although a fast-running river almost surrounded the site, it was in a deep gorge and could not be diverted as a small stream could. Drinking water eventually flowed in conduits from the surrounding hills. The rere-dorter at Durham pro-jected westwards on the river side of the dormitory. On the lower floor of the rere-dorter water flowed down a stone-lined drain. Above was a passageway and a series of small cubicles each with a seat over the drain. The arrangement worked well enough though the community may have suffered some inconvenience from the smell when a west wind blew.

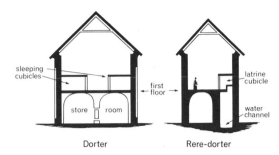

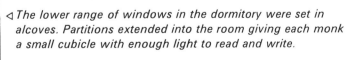

◁ *The lower range of windows in the dormitory were set in alcoves. Partitions extended into the room giving each monk a small cubicle with enough light to read and write.*

Although not the first one owned by the monks, this splendid clock, which shows the phases of the moon as well as the time, was built while Thomas Castell was prior (1494–1519). It was damaged in later years but has now been restored and stands in its original position in the south transept of the cathedral. ▷

Five monks singing at a feast-day service. One is wearing a cope decorated with crosses. They are reading the music from a big book on a lectern shaped like an eagle. This picture is from a famous fourteenth-century English manuscript known as the Luttrell Psalter.

Matins

When the signal was given at midnight for the service of Matins the monks had 'to rise without delay' – encouraging one another because the sleepy ones might make excuses – and make their way down to the cloister where they assembled for the procession into the church.

Once in choir (the part of the church near the altar, where the monks prayed), the sub-prior would give the signal to begin the long service of hymns and psalms and readings. If anyone was too late to come in the procession with the others he would have to come in alone and stretch himself out on the floor in the middle of the choir. This was a sign of apology for being late. The sub-prior would give a signal – probably a knock on the wood of his choir stall – and the latecomer could then get up and go to his place.

After the novices had been a while in the monastery they would be allowed to read or sing lessons and prayers. For those who had already been pupils in the song school, this would not be too difficult, but for a newcomer the first sound of his own voice singing alone in the great church must have been frightening.

When the service was over the monks went back to bed for a few more hours, only to be woken again about half past five for early morning prayers. At this service of Prime more prayers and hymns were sung, but not so many as at Matins.

After Prime there would be time to wash – in the conduit in the cloister, a cold business in winter – and to have a quick breakfast of bread and ale.

In the 1370s Lord John Neville gave the magnificent screen (or 'reredos') which still stands behind the high altar. It is made of stone from Caen in Normandy and was brought by sea to Newcastle, packed in boxes. In the niches stood 107 statues, destroyed in 1540. The drawing on the next page shows a modern artist's impression of the scene during a service in the fifteenth century.

Chapter

At about 9 o'clock the bells rang for the Chapter Mass. This was followed by Chapter, a meeting of all the monks, so called because a chapter of the Rule was read out. The meeting was held in the chapter house, a large room opening off the east cloister. The monks sat on benches around the walls, each in his own place with the juniors near the door and the prior in a special seat opposite the door (see the drawing on page 41).

This meeting was a council for deciding all the important questions in the life of the community. Monks were appointed, for several years at a time, to carry out certain duties. Jobs that came up only occasionally – preparing for a special festival, entertaining important guests, taking over from someone who was ill – could be decided on the spot. The sub-prior would deal with these and make any announcements. At other times there would be business discussions, about the general state of the finances, or about the sale of monastic property, or the admission of young monks.

Sometimes a monk would be accused of breaking the Rule. He would have to stand in the middle of the room while the prior or sub-prior corrected him and pronounced some punishment. The punishments were listed in the Rule and included penalties like a diet of bread and water, or being excluded from the company of the other monks for a certain time. Really serious offenders might be condemned to the priory prison.

The Chapter was held in an orderly fashion with the prior or his deputy in charge. No one was supposed to speak out when another monk was speaking. If a monk had something to say he would stand up and wait until the prior gave the signal to speak. The meetings were important in keeping everyone in touch with what was going on, and in keeping order in the priory.

The eastern alley of the cloister. At the far end is the prior's door into the cathedral. A drawing adapted from a nineteenth-century engraving.

On special feast days rich robes were worn at the services in the cathedral. This cope, or cloak, is made of Florentine cloth-of-gold. The border at the top shows scenes from the Passion of Christ. The cope was probably made late in the fifteenth century.

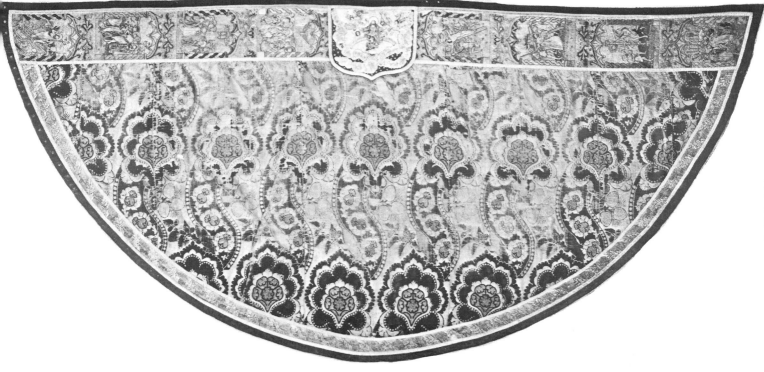

High Mass

It seems, from what is known of the timetable at Durham in the fifteenth century, that the monks would not have much time to themselves during the whole morning – that is if they attended all the services. The novices were certainly supposed to go, but monks who had other important work to do would have been excused from some services.

At 11 o'clock the High Mass was celebrated at the main altar in the cathedral. This was carried out with special solemnity as you can see in the picture opposite. The people from the town came, especially on the great festivals. There would be music (sung by the boys of the choir school, as well as by the monks), incense, elaborately embroidered robes and hangings, and rich gold or silver vessels on the altar. There were other Masses, too, of less solemnity. Most of the monks eventually became priests and would celebrate special Masses every day, often for the souls of the dead. These Masses were said earlier in the morning at smaller altars around the cathedral, especially in the Chapel of the Nine Altars which was built in the thirteenth century to give space for many Masses.

Dinner

Dinner was served after High Mass. When the bell was rung those who were to eat in the refectory gathered in the cloister and washed their hands in the basin provided around the conduit, which supplied clean running water. When all were ready they walked in procession up the stairs to their places in the refectory. Grace was sung. Then the monks sat in silence at long tables while the food was passed round by the servers. During the meal one monk, sitting in a special high seat, or pulpit, read aloud from the Bible, or the lives of the saints (especially St Cuthbert) or the writings of holy men.

The meal probably consisted of soup – one kind only – bread, and a dish of vegetables. Meat and fish were allowed only on special days but cheese, eggs and fruit were often served. All this was washed down with ale, the main drink which was served with every meal. At the end of the meal a signal was given. Grace was sung again and the monks left the refectory. Those who had been appointed for the week to serve at table, or read, or help in the kitchen, had their meals at a 'second table' afterwards. Meanwhile, the others walked in procession to the cemetery to pray for the dead.

Not everyone took meals in the main refectory. Those who were elderly or ill ate in the hall of the infirmary. So did some of the officials of the monastery, perhaps because the food was better and the meal less formal. By the fifteenth century it was also more common for many monks to take their meals in the room called the 'loft' where they probably enjoyed the conversation of their friends. Or they might be invited to dine in the prior's hall and help to entertain the guests.

After dinner there was some free time when the monks could rest on their beds or read. Then followed more prayers, but also some time for work. A light meal was served about 6 o'clock in the evening. About 7, the evening prayer (called Compline) was sung in the church. Afterwards the monks went to bed. At least they were supposed to, though there were complaints to the bishop that during the long summer evenings some would be found walking in the garden, laughing and talking after Compline.

The great octagonal kitchen at Durham was built between 1366 and 1374. Inside are five big fireplaces. The photograph on the right shows how the kitchen towers above the more modern rooms built beside it.

below: The unique stone vault of the kitchen roof designed by the master mason, John Lewyn.

△ The hatch in the lobby near the door of the refectory. Food from the kitchen nearby was passed through the hatch and carried to the tables by those appointed to serve at the meal.

The career of a monk

The young monk could expect to follow this daily routine for the rest of his life. But the work he did in the time available between the church services would change.

For the first six years, his time would mostly be taken up with studies. Some of these might be done outside Durham altogether, for he could be sent for a few years to Oxford where the monks had their own college.

Later, the bishop would make him a priest and he could take his place as a fully-fledged monk, no longer under supervision as a novice.

Even so, a Durham monk was encouraged to continue his studies all his life. He had the use of one of the best collections of books in the north of England (see chapter 3).

He was also expected to take his share of the daily work of running the monastery. In a big priory like Durham there was much to do. It was like a highly organised 'corporation' with monk 'officials' in charge of the different 'departments'. Other monks acted as assistants to the officials and helped to supervise the servants.

The running of the monastery can be divided into discipline, or supervising the religious life, and supply, or getting and spending.

The prior was head of the whole priory and he decided what everyone else had to do. He had a council of senior monks to advise him. Second in command was the sub-prior, who took over and acted for the prior when the prior was away. The following lists show the other officials at Durham in November 1416.

In charge of discipline

TITLE	NAME	WHAT HE DID
Sub-prior	Robert Ripon	Second-in-command to the prior
Third prior	Robert Crayk	Third-in-command after prior and sub-prior
Deans of order	John Durham, senior Thomas Moreby	Saw that all the monks attended services and other duties
Precentor	Hugh Werkworth	In charge of church music and ceremonies
Chancellor and Sacrist	John Wessington	In charge of the library, and the secretarial office. As sacrist he looked after the fabric of the church
Sub-sacrist	John Durham, junior	Helped the sacrist, especially in providing everything needed for church services
Feretrar	Robert Crayk (also third prior above)	In charge of St Cuthbert's shrine
Keeper of the Galilee Chapel	Henry Feriby	In charge of the chapel at the west end of the cathedral which included St Bede's shrine

In charge of supply

TITLE	NAME	WHAT HE DID
Bursar	William Drax	In charge of all money and supplies
Cellarer	John Lethom	In charge of supplies of meat and victuals
Terrar and Hostillar	William Barry	Land agent, and, as hostillar, in charge of the guest house
Chamberlain	Stephen Howden	In charge of the monks' clothes
Refectorian	Roger Langchester	In charge of the refectory, or dining hall
Commoner	William Graystanes	Supplied the monks 'commons', i.e. any extras to what was provided in the general way for all
Master of the Infirmary	Robert Eseby	Looked after the sick or old monks
Almoner	John Gisburn	In charge of alms generally and of the almonry schools

There was usually also a *Granator* who looked after supplies of grain, wheat, barley and rye – but he is not mentioned in this list.

In 1416 there were sixty-nine monks living either in Durham itself or in one of their other houses. At least thirty monks at any one time had special responsibilities or 'offices'.

In the course of his life, a monk would probably move from one job to another, or even from house to house. He could get wide experience in the management of men and business affairs. There was even the possibility that, as prior of Durham, he might become one of the most influential men in the north of England.

A typical career is that of the monk Richard Barton, who was ordained priest in 1412 and went immediately to Durham College, Oxford. Three years later he was sent to Stamford. By the 1420s he was back in Oxford for further studies and from 1428 to 1431 he was warden of Durham College, Oxford. Then he held various 'offices' at Durham: third prior, feretrar, and chamberlain. In May 1440 he was appointed prior of Stamford and he stayed there until he retired finally to Durham in 1462.

The life of a monk combined continual prayer and study, with many hours in the church every day, with the activities and responsibilities of something very like a business career. In the following chapters you can look at these different aspects of the monk's life in greater detail.

A twelfth-century manuscript in the monks' library has a list of 'remedies, medicines and charms'. It has pictures like this one showing cautery with a red hot needle. Below, a man heats more irons in a fire. One monk, the master of the infirmary, looked after the welfare of his ill brethren in a separate building, the monastic infirmary. Some sick and elderly lay men and women were given beds in another infirmary near the priory gates.

3 Books and learning

If prayer was to be the most important element in the monk's life – and many hours a day were spent in the church services – study and 'holy reading', or *lectio divina*, were needed to 'feed' his life of prayer.

This may have been the main reason for the emphasis placed on study and learning, but since the early days of the Benedictine monasteries, when they were the only centres of culture in the upheaval which followed the barbarian migrations, there had been a great tradition of monastic learning. It was in the libraries of the monasteries that the books of the great writers of the Classical World, and of the early Fathers of the Church, were preserved.

Durham priory was no exception. Although many of the

This drawing from a twelfth-century manuscript shows a monk writing with a quill pen. His paper rests on a board attached to his chair. In his left hand he holds a burnisher for pressing and polishing the gold leaf on ornamental letters.

books belonging to the old monasteries of Lindisfarne and Chester-le-Street had been lost in the years of wandering, some had survived and were carefully preserved by the Durham monks. Among their greatest treasures was the beautiful eighth-century book of Gospels from Lindisfarne. There was another Gospel book thought to have been written by Bede, and a copy of the Commentary of Cassiodorus on the Psalms. When the monks came to Durham, Bishop William of St Calais gave them forty-nine new books brought from the monasteries of Normandy and the south of England. These included the writings of many of the Fathers of the Church: Jerome, Augustine, Gregory and Ambrose. By the middle of the twelfth century there were 436 volumes in the library including Aesop's Fables, Homer and Plato, some Latin classics, and seven books on medicine.

All these books were copied by hand, some by the monks themselves. Many were beautifully decorated with pictures. By 1400, when the library had many more volumes, some of the books were written by professional scribes outside the monastery. By the end of the fifteenth century printed books began to appear. There were now more books on theology and law, while the lists show that some of the older books had been lost.

Every monk had his own book of the Psalms. He might also have a few other books for his own use, but most volumes would be in the library under the charge of the monk appointed as chancellor. At first the books were kept in cupboards in the north cloister. Special wood-panelled cubicles, called carrells, were built in the cloister to provide privacy, and some protection from draughts, for those who wished to read and write.

In the west cloister were carrells for the novices who had their own chest of books. There were also service books in the church, books for those in the infirmary, and, near the door of the refectory, books to be read aloud at meals. The

far right: *The beginning of St John's Gospel from the* Book of the Gospels *written at Lindisfarne sometime between 698 and 721.*

right: *One of the greatest treasures in the monks' library was this copy of Bede's* Life of St Cuthbert. *King Athelstan had presented it to the community of St Cuthbert, in 934, while they were at Chester-le-Street. This painting from the book shows the King presenting his gift to St Cuthbert himself. It is now in Corpus Christi College, Cambridge.*

most valuable books were kept in the 'spendement', or treasury, a special storeroom for valuables off the west alley of the cloister.

Although the monks did begin to buy printed books, not many of their books were bought in the way a modern library regularly buys books. Books came as gifts, or were brought by a monk when he joined the monastery. Many came from Oxford where monks had acquired them during their studies. A monk often seems to have kept his books all his life and only left them to the priory's collection after he died.

The new library

After the cloisters had been rebuilt in 1414, Prior Wessington saw the opportunity to build a new reference library to house many of the books he had taken care of as chancellor. The new library was built over the parlour in the east cloister. It was a fine room 60 ft (20 metres) long by 16 ft (5 metres) wide and cost £90 to build. The books were kept in presses or lecterns placed parallel to the long walls. The mark on each book showed its proper place. (2a 3i A meant the first book

on the second shelf of the third press.) There were ten presses in the room, each shelf of a press holding about twenty-five volumes.

The books were arranged by subject. Especially large were the sections of the library devoted to:
The Bible and the Fathers of the Church
Texts of theology
History and lives of the saints
Canon (Church) law and civil law
The writings of the Greek philosopher Aristotle
The monks could read in the library or they could borrow books. And not only the Durham monks used the library. Books were borrowed by the bishops, and by clergy and laymen all over the north of England. Loans were made to monks living in other houses. Records of the loans in the form of an indenture (an agreement written twice on a sheet of paper or parchment and then cut with a jagged edge so that the pieces could be fitted together for proof) are still in the archives at Durham.

By the fifteenth century, the monks at Durham possessed at least a thousand books, nearly all of them in Latin.

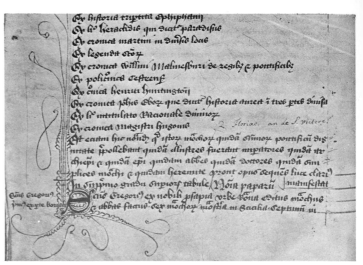

As chancellor (1407-16), John Wessington became familiar with the books in the library. Part of the list he made is shown here. It includes works by Bede, William of Malmesbury and Henry of Huntingdon, all famous medieval historians.

The 'spendement'. Valuables belonging to the monastery, or deposited by local gentry, were stored here. The shelves inside are modern but many of Durham's medieval manuscripts are still kept in this 'strong room'.

The Sunday sermon

As well as using the books for their own study, or lending them to others, the monks needed books to prepare for the sermons which they preached in the cathedral. Every Sunday at 12 noon the bell in the Galilee chapel was tolled for forty-five minutes, and then rung for fifteen minutes, 'so that all people of the town might have warning to come and hear the word of God preached'. From 'one of the clock until 3' the sermon was preached by a monk from a pulpit at the west end of the Galilee chapel. Many of the sermons would tell the stories of the life of Christ from the Gospels. Behind the preacher, in the glowing colours of the west windows were scenes of the Coming of the Wise Men, the Crucifixion, the Crowning of the Virgin Mary, and the saints of Durham, Cuthbert and Aidan, Bede and Oswald.

The schools

Near the priory gate was the almonry school where poor children from the town, as well as the sons of gentry families, were taught grammar. The school master was not a monk but a cleric appointed by the prior and paid forty shillings a year. By the sixteenth century there were thirty scholars. Some of the children lived in the town and came every day to school. Others lived in the priory. All had their meals from the monks' kitchen.

There was also a small song school where about eight boys were taught by a choirmaster. The prior of Durham also had to appoint masters of two schools in Yorkshire, one at Howden and one at Northallerton – both founded by a bishop of Durham.

The monks themselves often suggested that a boy, probably a relative, be given a place in one of the schools. Sometimes powerful landowners in the district recommended boys for the school. When his schooling was finished a boy might ask to become a monk. Or he might be given a scholarship to the monks' college at Oxford.

Durham College, Oxford

If a young monk showed special promise he, too, could be sent to Oxford for further studies. Durham monks had gone to Oxford university since about 1280 but it was only in 1381 that the bishop of Durham, Thomas Hatfield, established a regular academic college for them at Oxford. The priory was fortunate in having as one of its members a famous scholar, Uthred of Boldon, whose reputation helped to get the new college established. Bishop Hatfield left £3000 to support eight monks at the Oxford college. They were to be under the authority of a warden appointed by the prior at Durham. The Oxford monks continued all the services of the Church, just as at Durham, but they also studied in the university, reading philosophy and theology.

In 1405 a new building was begun with a chapel, a library and other rooms, around a quadrangle. Some remains of Durham College can still be seen today in the central quadrangle of the present Trinity College, Oxford, founded on the same site in 1555. In 1416 the college was the most important and prosperous of all the Durham houses.

Of the 132 monks who joined the community at Durham between 1383 and 1441, at least fifty-one went to Oxford. Some studied for four or five years and took the degree of Bachelor of Theology. Some did not stay long enough to take a degree; others stayed on for many years, living the life of a scholar. Only a few became doctors of theology, partly because taking the doctorate was an expensive and lengthy course involving the giving of a special feast to the university.

Monks who had taken Oxford degrees went back to important positions in Durham priory. All the priors from 1416 to 1539 were Oxford men. The establishment of Durham College thus had an important effect on Durham priory itself. Not only were there monks well equipped to look after their estates, and business and legal affairs, but also to entertain guests who might be among the highest in the land. The existence of the Oxford college had a lot to do with the high regard for learning in the priory itself. By the fifteenth century, Durham priory can perhaps be considered as a 'little university'.

An engraving, made in Germany in 1508, shows the progress of a medieval student's education. 'Grammar' is shown as a woman holding out to a boy the letters of the alphabet while she unlocks the door to the tower of knowledge. Inside are those who represent the other branches of study that led to a university degree. In the lower rooms Donatus and Priscian represent the Latin grammar books which all pupils had to study. Higher up are Aristotle (Logic), Cicero (Rhetoric), Boethius (Arithmetic), Pythagoras (Music), Euclid (Geometry) and Ptolemy (Astronomy). Then come Seneca (Moral Philosophy), an unnamed person for Physical Philosophy or Science, and over all, at the top of the tower, Peter Lombard who symbolizes Theology and Metaphysics. The few men who reached the top had completed the whole of the course of medieval studies.

4   Founding new houses

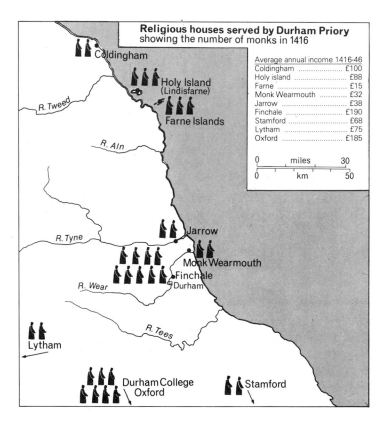

Religious houses served by Durham Priory
showing the number of monks in 1416

Average annual income 1416-46	
Coldingham	£100
Holy island	£88
Farne	£15
Monk Wearmouth	£32
Jarrow	£38
Finchale	£190
Stamford	£68
Lytham	£75
Oxford	£185

Not all monks in fifteenth-century England lived in great monasteries like Durham priory. In hundreds of smaller houses all over the country many monks lived much simpler, and often poorer, lives in groups of ten or twelve. Some houses might even have only two or three monks.

Many small houses depended on one of the great monasteries. Durham priory had nine of these *cellae* (cells) or daughter houses – more than most other English monasteries. The map shows where they were. The table suggests the

annual income (compare this with the income of Durham priory on page 36). All the cells were founded between the eleventh and thirteenth centuries, some on the sites of ancient monasteries. By the fifteenth century most were in financial difficulties.

The monks living in these houses had all been trained at Durham priory. Some had studied at Oxford. Then they were transferred, by the prior, to one of the cells for a few years, or – if all went well – for a longer time. But as few monks wanted to leave Durham, the prior had a continual problem in finding enough men to keep the cells going.

Why did they not want to go? Was it too lonely living in a small house with only two or three companions after years in the big community at Durham? The cells were often poor. Food might be scanty, and buildings cold and uncomfortable. There would be few books, or even no library at all. They would miss the splendour of the services in the cathedral. The neighbours could cause a lot of trouble. A spell in a small house could easily come to seem like a punishment for a monk who fell out of favour with his superiors. Priors must often have been tempted to exile the trouble makers and the misfits to other houses. This probably led to peace in Durham itself, but it can hardly have led to happy communities in the daughter houses.

Thomas Partrike at Lytham

Of course some monks *liked* to live away from Durham and spent many years happily in one of these outposts. There would be freedom from the discipline of routine in the mother house. If there happened to be a good cook, a few comfortable rooms, and friends among the local gentry, it could be a very pleasant life. Indeed one prior of Lytham in the fifteenth century, Thomas Partrike, enjoyed his independence so much that in 1442 he applied to Rome for permission to remain prior there until his death. This led to strong protests and legal action by Prior Wessington of Durham who saw his authority threatened. The Lytham house could be lost to Durham altogether if Partrike was allowed to have his own way. This would not only be a threat to the authority of the mother house. Revenues at Durham would suffer also. Even though the cells were often poor, they were expected to send an annual sum of money to Durham. Between 1415 and 1436 an expensive building programme at Durham – a new library,

Jarrow and Monk Wearmouth
Both famous monasteries in Saxon times (see page 9). Never really recovered after twenty-three monks went to the new Durham priory in 1083. Refounded, but little expansion after that period.

Holy Island or Lindisfarne
Famous as the monastery of St Aidan and St Cuthbert (see page 5). A large church, but short of money and liable to damage in Anglo–Scottish wars. Fortified by English in the fourteenth century.

Farne Island
Site of St Cuthbert's hermitage (see page 5). After 1150, monks from Durham went there as hermits. A few were famous as very holy men – others lived scandalously. Always very poor.

Stamford (Lincolnshire)
Founded about 1146. Maintained a tradition of scholarship and study until the fourteenth century when its numbers decreased. Useful as a base for collecting Durham's revenues in the south of England.

Coldingham
Founded in the twelfth century. One of the richest monasteries in Scotland, although the monks sent from Durham were English. A long struggle to maintain their position during Anglo–Scottish wars eventually failed with the expulsion of English monks in 1478.

Lytham (Lancashire)
Founded in the twelfth century. At first prosperous but failure to keep on good terms with local Lancastrian gentry made it an unpopular house for Durham monks.

Durham College, Oxford
Founded as a house of study for Durham Monks (see page 29).

Finchale
Originally the cell of St Godric, a twelfth-century hermit. By the fifteenth century one of the wealthiest of the cells and a holiday house for monks from durham.

The ruins of the large priory church of Holy Island, or Lindisfarne, off the Northumbrian coast. All of the ruined buildings you can see are of the period when the priory was staffed by a group of Durham monks. Notice how the medieval parish church, still in use, was built just outside the west front of the monks' church. As at Finchale priory (see page 32), the monastic quarters were remodelled when numbers fell in the later Middle Ages.

repairs to the infirmary and to the central tower of the cathedral, and new apartments for the prior – were paid for partly out of funds from the cells. This was not unreasonable when the mother house trained the monks and took care of them in old age. But it is not surprising that a man like Partrike objected and tried to separate Lytham from such 'taxes'.

He refused to acknowledge the authority of the prior of Durham and refused to come to the annual meeting of the heads of the cells at Durham on the Monday after Ascension Day.

Prior Wessington asked for help from the bishop and then sent a messenger, one Thomas Clough, to Lytham. Partrike met Clough in the orchard and threatened him, refusing to accept the letters he carried. Next morning Partrike put his words into effect. Three armed men advanced upon poor Clough and threatened him with weapons drawn. If he persisted in offering his letters they would make him eat the letters, and the box he carried them in. Clough gave way and left.

The long legal struggle that followed was won by Durham priory, although Partrike had the support of leading Lancashire families like the Stanleys. In 1446 Partrike had to go and live at Durham again. Here he complained, not surprisingly, that the prior 'luffyd me never and Robert Westmorland and John Gatishead and Richard Bell are cheff wit hym, and none of them luffis me'. In 1450 he seems to have left Durham priory altogether. But the glory of St Cuthbert had been saved and Saint Cuthbert's inheritance protected. Although some monasteries lost their daughter houses, Durham lost only one – Coldingham, to the Scots in the 1470s.

Finchale

Two houses were an exception to the general unpopularity of the cells. Durham College had its own special attraction as a house of study. There was never any difficulty in finding monks to go to Oxford.

Nor was there a shortage of monks willing to live at Finchale. This house, only an hour's ride from Durham itself, was one of the wealthiest cells. In fact its situation was so attractive that it became something of a holiday house for the Durham monks. As well as the seven or eight who lived there regularly, parties of another half a dozen monks might be sent for a stay of three weeks or so. It was a pleasant place for a sick monk to recuperate – or for a monk who had held a high position in Durham to enjoy a comfortable old age.

During the fifteenth century the buildings, especially the living quarters of the monks, were made more comfortable. Although Finchale priory is in ruins, it still gives a good idea of the smaller type of monastic establishment.

5 Getting and spending

The annual income

The main part of the priory's income came from its lands. Even before the foundation of Durham priory in 1083, gifts had been made to 'the community of St Cuthbert' of manors, estates and farms in the north of England. The map shows where these were. The monks farmed some of the manors themselves; others were let to tenants who gave, instead of money, corn and other produce. At first goods were supplied directly to the priory but by the fifteenth century it was more usual for the monks' agent, or 'reeve', to sell the produce in the local market and send money to the priory.

Durham Priory's churches
• Church under the patronage of Durham Priory in the later Middle Ages

Manors of Durham Priory

• Major manors shown thus

Another part of the income came from tithes. Over the centuries, churches in the north of England had also been 'given' to the priory. By this means, a powerful lord, or an abbot, would become the patron of a parish church and control the appointment of the priest. If the monastery 'appropriated' this church, it then had the right to the tithes (or tenths) of farm produce. This often happened in the case of Durham's churches. Here too it was usual for the monks' agent to sell the produce and send money to the priory. The second map shows how many parish churches or 'benefices' were under the patronage of Durham priory. Other contributions also came from the small houses of monks founded from Durham, as seen in chapter 4.

The priory also owned woodland and mines. Timber and coal were mostly produced for its own use. Deep coal mining was not possible because the difficulties of draining water out of deep mines had not been solved; but some coal and timber was sold, and several mines leased.

The table on page 36 shows the total income for the year 1420 and how it was divided among the various officials of the priory. (Amounts of money are given in old-style currency: 12 pence in a shilling and 20 shillings in a pound.) The map below shows where some of the everyday supplies came from.

Spending

It is not easy to show exactly what all the expenses of the priory were but from the bursar's account rolls of 1422–3 we can get the following impression:

Expenses 1422–3	£	s	d
Cloth, from merchants in York	52	13	9
Red and white wine, from merchants in Newcastle	56	0	0
Horse-shoeing, including the iron	45	0	0
Horse fodder	50	0	0
Repairs to property	60	0	0
Salaries, pensions and wages	100	0	0
Travelling expenses (and other)	34	0	0
Prior's expenses	11	9	11
Alms and gifts	15	14	11½
Rent and allowances	25	0	0
Contributions to Church taxation	23	0	0
TOTAL	£482	18	7½

To this total must be added:

Annual average expense of £390 for:

sheep – bought for slaughter	fish	cheese
	poultry	butter
cattle	eggs	
pigs		

Annual average £400 spent on grain:
370 quarters of wheat or rye
1200 quarters of barley

Most of the barley was malted and made into ale.

This gives total expenses of £1272.18.7½

In a typical week 19–25 July 1432 there were eaten at Durham

5 cattle	2 calves	13 piglets	and one cart
22 sheep	22 hens	400 eggs	load of fish

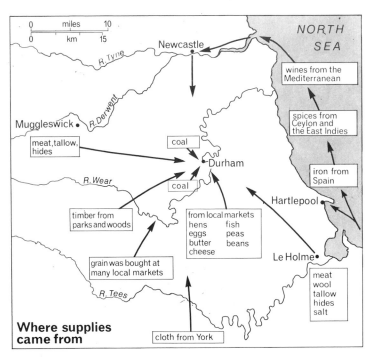

Where supplies came from

A map of the County of Durham,
published by Christopher Saxton
in 1576.

Estimate of annual income in 1420

OFFICIAL	ESTIMATED INCOME		
	£	s	d
Bursar	1500		
	(from rents about £1000		
	from tithes about £500)		
Hostillar	170		
Almoner	100		
Chamberlain	100		
Sacrist	66	13	4 (100 marks)
Commoner	66	13	4 (100 marks)
Feretrar	30		
Terrar	20		
	£2053	6	8

The list on page 24 explains each official's job. The table shows that the bursar who had to supply all the food had by far the largest income.

The bursar

Part of St Benedict's ideal (and of the Christian ideal) was that a monk (or any Christian) was happier if he did not own too many things, and was not always looking for more. If you are content with having only what you really need, you are more free to think about other people, and to think about God. Though the monastery as a whole should be able to support itself – and so could own land, buildings, animals and so on – the individual monk did not own anything. He simply asked for what he needed and was given what he asked for. This worked well if the officials were what St Benedict said they should be. But everyone could be miserable if those in charge of supplies were greedy for themselves or showed favouritism.

Even in St Benedict's time one monk was given special charge of supplies. He was called the 'cellarer'. The Rule says 'Let there be chosen out of the community, as cellarer of the monastery, a wise man, and of mature character, temperate, not a great eater, not haughty or headstrong, not offensive, not dilatory, nor wasteful but a God-fearing man, who may be like a father to the whole community.'

An initial letter in a thirteenth-century French manuscript shows a monk cellarer tasting the wine he is drawing from a cask. Perhaps the artist who drew the picture envied the monk who had the opportunity to help himself.

The business of providing everything needed for thirty or forty monks was always demanding but in earlier times it was at least straightforward. At first the monks grew their own grain and vegetables on their own land. They made their own ale, kept fish in their stream, ate little meat, made their clothes from the wool of their own sheep. There was little business done with people outside the monastery. But by the fifteenth century, life was more complex both inside and outside a monastery. More people lived in towns, goods were bought and sold with money and traded over long distances. There was now a whole class of people, the merchants, who made a living from trade.

As well as this, as we have already seen, Durham priory itself was a much bigger organization. It supported forty monks and many servants. Guests and travellers were cared for in the guest hall, children were looked after and educated in the school. The priory had responsibilities for daughter houses, lands, and tenants, scattered across the greater part of the north of England.

Retired servants and elderly relatives of the monks were cared for in the priory's 'hospitals' or almshouses. Two of these almshouses, one near Gilesgate on the outskirts of Durham, and the other a few miles away at Witton Gilbert, each housed five men or women. In the city itself the priory supported two infirmaries caring for a total of forty-three inmates, some of them elderly married couples.

It is estimated that the priory fed, in all, 300 people every day.

This meant much more work than St Benedict had planned for his cellarer. By the fifteenth century, in many big abbeys, the cellarer looked after food supplies, but the responsibility for the money affairs of the whole establishment was given to a new official, the bursar.

He had a whole team of officials to help him look after money and supplies. Even so the monks at Durham thought the bursar's job was too much for one man. Priors had great difficulty finding anyone to take it on. For instance, between 1419 and 1432, the prior tried out three monks. None of them was very successful. Buildings were neglected, food was wasted, and debts were not paid. Then in the autumn of 1432, in desperation, the prior appointed Thomas Lawson, a young monk who had been cellarer for the past four years. The prior soon realized that this appointment was a disastrous mistake.

The story of Thomas Lawson

Each year at Whitsuntide the bursar had to draw up accounts for the whole year. These accounts were written on both sides of five or six pieces of parchment. The pieces were then stitched together head to tail in a long strip which could be made into one roll. The accounts listed money received and given out to the officials. Three copies were made. Several senior monks were appointed to inspect the accounts and report to the annual meeting of all the monks in June.

When Whitsun 1433 came, Brother Thomas complained that he had not had time to draw up the rolls. The more the prior insisted, the more anxious Thomas became, until it is said he was on the point of committing suicide. Finally he did produce some accounts (and his account rolls for the next five years are still at Durham). But he 'cooked the books' in

A fifteenth-century box for storing the charters and account rolls concerning the estates belonging to the priory. As you can see, the monastic archives were carefully labelled and preserved.

that he did not record the debts that were mounting up. During the years that followed rumours spread that all was not well.

The terrar (see page 24 for what the terrar does), Henry Helay, and a clerk in the bursar's office eventually made a report of the true state of things. Debts of over £1210 had been concealed by Thomas Lawson.

At this time Thomas was inspecting the estates. It was the bursar's duty to pay regular visits to the priory's manors. He would discuss with his agent the state of the crops and check how many animals were kept. Sometimes he presided at the courts which were held to settle any grievances the tenants might have. The bursar needed to know how much money he would receive in the autumn from the sale of grain and animals on the manors.

When Thomas heard that the news had got out he left his lodgings in the middle of the night and went into hiding rather than go back to face the angry monks.

This left the prior with the problem of who was to take over – now especially difficult because things had got into

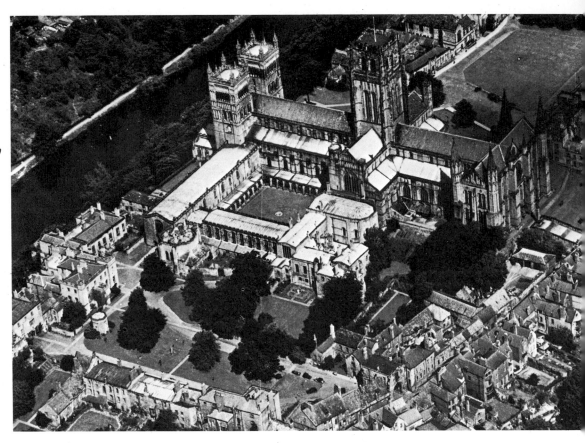

The photograph of Durham cathedral as it is today shows clearly the great courtyard, now called the college, which must have been the scene of so much activity in the days of the monks. Compare this with the plan on page 13. The storehouses, guest-house and infirmary have all been rebuilt as canons' houses; but look for the great kitchen, the prior's apartments and the gatehouse.

confusion. He tried to persuade various monks to take on the job but all flatly refused. Finally the bursar's work was divided up among several men. The experiment lasted for seven years but had disadvantages. Because no one had responsibility for keeping a check on money and supplies as a whole, the costs of the different departments kept creeping up.

Although Durham priory seemed to everyone to be rich and powerful (and there were some envious and critical comments), the monks themselves always watched their finances carefully. Compared with the earlier centuries, times were not good. An account of 1405 says that 'the goods, rents and income of the said monastery have been so notoriously wasted and diminished that they no longer suffice to pay the usual debts and support the convent in all its necessities'.

Income had dropped from £2200 a year in 1330–1 to £1470 in 1347–8 and it stayed at this lower level for a long time. There was little chance of increasing it. Wars with Scotland, plague, cattle disease and crop failures had all had their effect. New gifts of land or churches, such as had in earlier times built up the priory's resources, were no longer made. A monastery could not bring new lands into the family by the marriages of sons and daughters, as other landowners could. It was no wonder that the prior had such difficulty in finding a good bursar who could make ends meet.

Yet, although they may have *felt* insecure, if the monks managed for so long, and in difficult times, to provide for so many people, they can hardly be considered incompetent in organizing their financial affairs.

Much of their stability in the fifteenth century may also have been due to the man who was prior from 1416 to 1446, John Wessington.

6 Prior John Wessington

John Wessington was born about 1371 in the village of Wessington (later called Washington) in the county of Durham. His family were well-to-do and were later to become one of the most famous of the English gentry families. When he was about seventeen years old John joined the community at Durham priory. He was clothed and professed as a monk and spent several years in the training and studies as a novice. Then he was made a priest and sent to Durham College, Oxford. He did not take a University degree, but he stayed at the college for thirteen years. He must have had some talent for business and administration, because he became bursar of the college. He would thus have had a lot to do with the rebuilding that was going on at the time.

Chancellor

In 1407 he returned to live as an ordinary monk at Durham priory. He took his part in the services in the church and probably continued his studies in his spare time. He was particularly interested in the early history of the priory and read many of the vast collection of documents in the priory's archives. Quite soon after his return he was made chancellor (see p.24) and took over from Thomas Rome the charge of all documents and legal affairs. In the four centuries of its history the priory had been given many special privileges – grants of land, rights to income, permission to relax certain rules – by bishops, kings or popes, and all were carefully recorded. If, in later years, the monks were in danger of losing any privileges it was essential to have someone in the community who could produce the documents, argue their case, and defend the fame of St Cuthbert (for they regarded everything they had as their inheritance from St Cuthbert). Any injury *they* might suffer would also take away from the glory of their saint. Wessington was to be chancellor for nine years. For seven of these years he was also the sacrist of the cathedral.

Sacrist

In a cathedral priory the sacrist's job was very demanding. He was responsible for seeing that the great church building was kept in good repair. During the time (1409–16) that Wessington was sacrist there was no major rebuilding going on in the cathedral itself but he had to supervise the reconstruction of the cloister. He advised the masons about what was wanted, supervised the workers and kept accounts of wages and costs.

The sacrist also had to see that everything was ready for the services in the church and that the building was kept clean. As this was of course more work than one man could do, the sacrist had a team of helpers: a sub-sacrist (also a monk), and a crowd of servants who would sweep floors and lay clean rushes or straw, provide braziers of coal for heating in the winter, wash the linen, prepare candles and oil lamps, clean altar vessels and candlesticks. The elaborately embroidered robes worn during the ceremonies had to be stored carefully

In the roof of the cloister is a restored carved wooden boss with the Wessington family heraldic shield: argent, two bars gules, in chief three molets or. *Because President George Washington was a famous descendant of this family it used to be wrongly argued that the 'stars and stripes' of the United States of America were derived from these arms.*

left: *A twelfth-century manuscript from St Albans abbey shows a monk, perhaps the sacrist, with his key and money bag.*

far left: *In the passageway, or triforium, high above the side aisle of the cathedral the sacrist could inspect the roof timbers and watch out for any damage.(From a nineteenth-century engraving by R. W. Billings.)*

and put out ready for the services. Bread and wine, too, had to be supplied for Mass. The banners and crosses had to be put ready for processions. It was a job that needed someone who could pay attention to details, not get flustered, and work well with others. It seems clear that Wessington was good at all these.

The election

On 15 September 1416 Prior John Hemingburgh died. He had ruled the monastery for twenty-five years. A few days later, probably even before the late prior had been buried in the cathedral, the first steps were taken in the election of a new prior. Even though it was many years since the monks had elected a prior they knew what to do because the whole procedure of an election had been laid down in detail by the laws of the Church. First they had to tell the bishop that the prior was dead and ask permission to elect a new one. As it happened the bishop, Thomas Langley, had just gone to France. Thomas Ryhale was sent as messenger and caught up with him at Calais. The bishop wrote a letter to his own official at Durham instructing him to issue the licence for the election and affix the bishop's great seal. The priory had to pay 50 shillings for the document.

40

The licence was issued on 17 October. On the next day the monks met in council in the chapter house to set the date of the election as 5 November. Messengers set out immediately to notify all the monks living in the other houses and summon them to come. A few days later monks began to ride in from these houses. A large party of legal advisers arrived from York. By 5 November there were sixty-four monks and eight other witnesses present.

On the day itself a great crowd gathered. Many people in the town would be eager to know who would be the new prior. Besides, an election was a great occasion – so rare it might happen only once in a lifetime. A High Mass was sung in the cathedral. Then the bell was rung and all the monks went in procession to the chapter house. The sub-prior, Robert Rypon, preached a sermon, prayers were said for guidance and then all those who were not monks (except for the eight lawyers and witnesses) were sent out. The doors were locked. The sub-prior called the roll of monks and the lawyers checked that everything had been done as the Church laws said. All was ready. Then, as if at a signal, the monks stood up, all together, and called out the name of one monk: John Wessington. Wessington himself was left sitting in silence.

Of course if there had been any disagreement, or if there were several candidates proposed, the monks would have

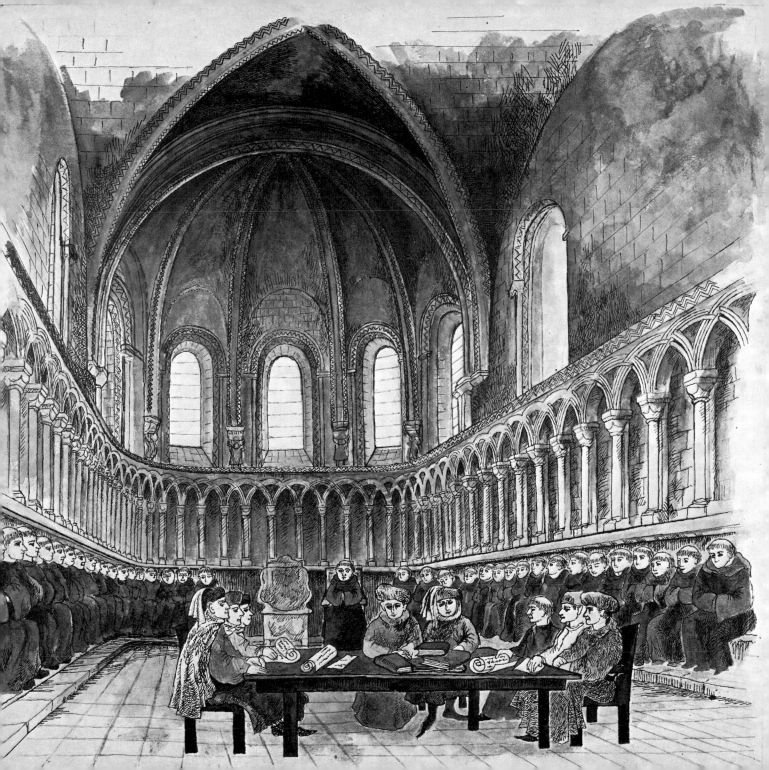

voted separately but this 'election by acclamation' was the quickest way when there was an obvious choice and the community were agreed beforehand.

The monks then went in procession from the chapter house to the high altar singing the hymn 'Te Deum'. One of the monks announced the result to the people waiting in the cathedral. Then Wessington was taken to the small chapel in the infirmary where he spent the night praying and trying to decide whether to accept the task of ruling the monastery. Next morning he accepted: 'for the honour of the Trinity, the Virgin Mary, Saint Cuthbert and All Saints'.

One more formality was necessary before the new prior could take his place in the church and chapter house. This was the approval of the bishop. As we have seen (page 9), the bishop had authority over the monks both as head of the diocese and as abbot of the monastery. Bishop Langley received a report of the election and satisfied himself that everything had been carried out according to the laws. Eventually on 22 December Wessington (who was ill at the time and could not travel) sent another monk, William Barry, to swear the oath of allegiance to the bishop at Howden, south of York, where he was spending Christmas. The bishop sent back two letters signed with his seal. One was to Wessington confirming his election. The other was to the community telling them to obey the new prior. Christmas celebrations in the priory that year were especially splendid.

What kind of a man should the prior be?

In the time between his election and his formal approval by the bishop Wessington must have thought often about the big responsibility he had accepted. St Benedict, when he wrote his Rule, laid great importance on the kind of man the abbot ought to be. Obviously if a group of men promise to live together for the rest of their lives, and to obey one man for the rest of *his* life, then the sort of person he is makes a great difference. If he is selfish and thoughtless, or throws his weight around, or goes off on long journeys, or spends all his time with the great lords of the district, then his monks will not be happy. They will not have a father. There will be no sense of living as a family.

St Benedict said that the abbot ought always to remember what he is called ('father') and live up to it. He must take care

of his monks (though not show favouritism), encourage them, correct them if they go astray, and show by his own life how they ought to live.

Above all he has to remember that even though he may become very powerful, his power is only so that he can help the monks to live up to their ideal of prayer and holiness. For this responsibility he will have to answer to God: 'And whatever may be the number of the brethren under his care, let him be certainly assured that on the Day of Judgement he will have to give an account to the Lord of all these souls, as well as his own.' The Rule also says that the abbot is not to command monks to do anything impossible!

In earlier days when monasteries were smaller and self-contained, the abbot lived more or less the same life as the monks. By the fifteenth century, as we have seen, the monastery was a large and wealthy institution, owning big estates and employing many servants. The prior of Durham was an important person in the land and could no longer live as a simple monk.

He did continue to attend the services in the church whenever he could. He came often to the daily meeting of the monks in the chapter house and appointed all the priory officials. On the great feast days he walked in the processions in the cathedral and the town, wearing his mitre and carrying a crozier – the symbols, usually, of a bishop but granted by the pope in recognition of the importance of the prior of Durham.

But there were many other duties to attend to, guests to entertain, tenants, messengers and clerks to be interviewed. To do all this properly the prior had come to need a special house of his own and many helpers.

The prior's household

John Wessington had not lived long in the prior's rooms at the south-east corner of the cloister before he set about improving the arrangements. He wanted rooms fit to entertain the greatest in the land. And because he could not spare much time to attend the usual activities of the monks, he wanted them to come to him – in groups for meals, or for recreation, or just to keep him in touch. This meant more building. Between 1424 and 1436 a completely new set of rooms was built for the prior. The accounts show that £300 was spent on

this building. At the height of the activity, twenty workmen, including three masons, worked full time. The wages bill was £50 a year.

There was no master mason as such. The prior and his chaplain Thomas Nesbitt directed the work themselves. In 1446 a list of the rooms in the prior's house included a chapel dedicated to St Nicholas, the prior's hall, his upper chamber and his lower chamber (bedrooms), a wine cellar, buttery and wardrobe. There were also smaller storerooms, offices, a study and a parlour.

The rooms were comfortable. There was glass in the windows, carved wooden ceilings, red hangings in the bedrooms, and, in the buttery, a valuable collection of silver including a salt cellar with a silver gilt cover, engraved with the prior's arms. In the chapel were embroidered vestments, and ornaments of gold, silver and precious stones.

The meals were more elaborate than those served to the other monks in the main refectory, although all the food was cooked in the same kitchen. The accounts show some of the

The prior in his parlour with his monk chaplain and lay steward. A modern artist's impression.

more exotic food ordered for the prior's table. Sweet wines, shipped from the Mediterranean, were bought in London. Oysters and salmon were sent down from Northumberland. Dishes were spiced with pepper, ginger, cinnamon, cloves or mace, and included figs, raisins, rice, dates, saffron and currants. The most expensive spices were cloves and mace which cost 3 shillings a pound in London. It is not surprising that the monks looked forward to an invitation to dine with the prior. Many other people also enjoyed visiting the prior, invited or not.

Guests

Since the time of St Benedict, monasteries have provided food and shelter for travellers. Visitors came on official business, as did Richard Bekyngham, a royal chancery clerk who was hoping to be appointed priest in one of the priory's parish churches. Some were on pilgrimage to the shrine of St Cuthbert. Others were wanting somewhere to spend a comfortable night on the long journey north to Scotland. Most visitors stayed in the guest hall under the care of the hostillar. The more important ones might be lodged in the bishop's castle or the prior's house. Although the prior lived in a style that was scarcely matched by any other household in the north, he kept more or less open house.

Again the monastic accounts show how expensive it all was. In 1444 Wessington calculated that he had spent £400 on hospitality for visitors staying on 'Scottish business'. Fighting between the Scots and the English was frequent and there were many attempts to arrange peace. In 1417–18 the duke of Exeter, the archbishop of York and their colleagues made an expedition north. Their stay at the priory cost £150. In 1424 James I, King of Scotland, stayed nearly two weeks discussing in the chapter house the terms of a proposed peace with English and Scottish lords. This cost the priory £100.

The Duke of Norfolk visited Durham five times in 1437–8, once staying for five days with a retinue of 300 men. In 1429 Cardinal Beaufort made two visits on his way to see King James. This time the accounts record only 26s 8d spent on linen and 13s 4d given to the Cardinal's cooks! In 1448, as we have seen, Henry VI of England stayed at the priory. Another famous visitor was Aeneas Sylvius who later became Pope Pius II. He had been visiting the Scottish king early in 1436 but he was so seasick on the way there that he decided to travel home by land, disguised as a merchant.

We do not know much about that visit but the records do help us to imagine one feast in the prior's hall. This was probably in 1441 and a rough plan of the seating arrangements has survived. There were twenty-six guests, chief of whom were the bishop, and the abbots of Newminster and Blanchland in Northumberland. The prior's steward William Hoton (see opposite) was there and so were the bishop's steward, the sheriff and other officials. Then there were eight university graduates, the deans and rectors of the most important churches in the diocese. Some Durham monks were at the feast, too, but the plan shows them seated at a separate table. From what we know of Wessington he seems to have been more at home in the company of churchmen like this than with the great lords who visited him.

The prior also had to entertain messengers from the king

Musicians. From a thirteenth-century Spanish manuscript.

and the lords, or agents, officials and lesser gentry, or travelling players who moved from one great house to another. As it was usual for the players to amuse the company after dinner, their visits must have made the monastic feasts especially lively, though when the prior was criticized about this he said he would be only too pleased to stop it – he was not much interested in such shows himself and only put them on because it was the custom.

The prior's helpers

To assist him in the complicated business of running his own household as well as the affairs of the priory, the prior had many helpers. Some were monks, others laymen employed by the prior. There were two chaplains, who were monks.

One chaplain acted as a personal assistant to the prior, saying Mass and praying with him, writing letters as his secretary and keeping the prior's seal.

The other chaplain was the prior's main financial agent, his 'monk-steward'. This official had to order all the supplies for the household. He had to send the bills to the bursar of the monastery, though he did have some income for the prior's household from sales of coal and timber. The monk-steward also had to see that the prior's rooms, furniture, linen and clothing were kept in good order. He had to supervise and pay the other household servants. While the first chaplain might be a young monk, the steward was usually an older man as this was a much more responsible post.

A third important member of the prior's household was the lay steward.

William Hoton, the prior's lay steward

William Hoton, of Hardwick Hall in the Stockton Ward of County Durham, belonged to one of the gentry families of the north but had no son to succeed him. He was already steward to the second earl of Westmorland. It was this family, the Nevilles (who were on good terms with the priory), who recommended that Wessington should make Hoton his lay steward. This he did in 1437 and Hoton remained steward until he died in 1446. The steward's duties were set out in his letters of appointment. He was to assist the prior and the bursar in the administration of all the priory's manors. He had to preside three times a year, with two monks, at the prior's manor courts, and examine the terms on which monastic land was leased to tenants.

This was an important responsibility and some stewards took the opportunity to give preference to their own relations. At Durham, though, the steward was clearly a paid servant of the prior and always had to act at the prior's direction. He was well paid. He received the highest wages paid by the priory, £5 a year from the prior and another 5 marks (about £3. 6s and 8d) from the terrar. The steward was even in a position to lend money to the monks. It is recorded that they owed him £60.

The lay steward also had to act as witness to much of the prior's official business, to attend when tenants came to pay their respects to the prior, and to advise on any problems that arose about sales of land. Because he lived nearby (and kept his own horses in the monastery stable), Hoton would often act as a messenger to the local gentry to settle some business matter. Sometimes he went to London to buy cloth, spices or wine for the prior.

When Holton died in 1446, the prior wrote that this death was 'the most heaviness and loss of one that ever befell to us or to the monastery of Durham'. This did not prevent the prior from arranging, the very next day, for a new steward.

The prior's counsellors

It was usual for the prior to have a group of experienced and influential laymen to advise him about the priory business.

In the parish church of Sedgefield in County Durham is a memorial to William Hoton, steward to the prior of Durham. It consists of a brass helmet with a crest of trefoils and scalloped 'mantling'. Below is an inscription recording his death in September 1445. In fact he died in 1446.

They were paid a pension, or 'retainer', as we would say. Wessington increased the numbers on his council from four to eight soon after his election. The men he chose were wealthy landowners, usually with some legal training and experience in the royal courts or the bishop's courts. Robert Rodes, who later became lay steward, was the priory's man in Westminster, acting as a link with parliamentary circles. Another was Robert Whelpington, the member of parliament for Newcastle and later its mayor. The prior also kept an official representative, a sergeant-in-law, at the Westminster law courts, an attorney at the royal exchequer to look after the payment of taxes, and an attorney in the bishop's court at Durham. There were also churchmen, trained in law at Oxford, to advise him in the complex affairs of Church law. The prior kept a group of these at the archbishop's court in York – again by payment of an annual pension – and even an agent at the papal court in Rome.

The employment of so many experts was very expensive. But the monks felt it was worth it. Business and legal affairs had become much more complicated. The monks could not compete with the professionals. Their solution, to call upon the help, as they needed it, of this network of contacts, worked out well enough in practice and kept them in touch with the centres of power both as regards the State and the Church.

The prior resigns

John Wessington continued as prior until 1446 when he was seventy-four, but during the last six years he was often ill. He found it increasingly difficult to carry on the business of the priory and finally, on 8 June 1446, he resigned. He had ruled the monastery for twenty-nine years. Only one other prior had ever served so long a term.

The community continued to treat him with honour and gave him a special suite of rooms in the monastic infirmary as well as a set of apartments at Finchale. He had five attendants, a chaplain, an esquire, a clerk, a valet and a boy, and an annual pension of £40.

Five years later 'exhausted by severe illness' the ex-prior was given the last sacraments of the Church and died on Good Friday, 1451. He was almost eighty years old.

Just as one monastery may be typical of many, so the life of one monk may tell us about the others. John Wessington's long career helps to answer some of the questions asked earlier in this book.

The death of a prior. Monks gather round his bedside praying and singing. The prior, wearing his mitre and black robe, lies with joined hands. The picture is from a fifteenth-century Durham manuscript known as an 'obit roll'. This was an announcement of a prior's death which was carried around to other monasteries in England to request their prayers for him. (The picture on the back cover of this book is from the same roll.)

7 The last days of Durham priory

When John Wessington resigned in 1446, William of Ebchester was elected prior of Durham. The daily routine of prayer and work continued, as it had done for nearly 400 years. There was no reason for anyone to expect a change. Yet, after William of Ebchester, there were to be only six more priors of Durham. Within a hundred years the monks themselves, and all the ancient ceremony surrounding the shrine of St Cuthbert – reminders of the earliest days of the Christian faith in Northumbria – were gone.

There is not room in this book to describe the events which led to the dissolution, as it is called, of the monasteries in England. Nor is there agreement today about why it happened. As we have seen, the questions about why men became monks, whether it was a worthwhile thing to do, whether they lived up to their ideal, cannot be easily answered, perhaps not even by the monks themselves. It is especially difficult for others to answer them hundreds of years later.

You can read elsewhere about the reformation in religion that was spreading across Europe and into England where King Henry had further reasons of his own for investigating the state of the monasteries.

The kings of England had concerned themselves closely with the affairs of the Church before Henry VIII's time. (They often appear in the story of Durham priory.) Kings had founded monasteries, visited them, held inquiries and suggested changes. This was done with the approval of the Church. So when, in the 1530s, the king began to inquire into the affairs of the monasteries, the monks may not at first have been alarmed.

First the king ordered that, in the interests of more economic running, as well as to encourage a better practice of religious life, all monasteries with an income of less than £200 a year should be closed. Durham priory had to close down nearly all its daughter houses. The monks returned to live at Durham, making a total of sixty-six in the priory at the Dissolution.

This great royal seal, partly damaged, was used by King Henry VIII for charters involving the Church. It is attached to a document in the Durham cathedral archives.

Soon after, the king, perhaps realizing the wealth that could be his if the big monasteries were closed too, set a more drastic plan in action. His chief minister, Thomas Cromwell, had sent commissioners to every religious house in England, to report on their property and to record any evil practices the monks might be guilty of.

At Durham three commissioners, Dr Leigh, Dr Henley and Dr Blitheman, with jewellers to help them, went through the vast treasure that had been given over the centuries by

47

pilgrims to the shrine of St Cuthbert. All precious jewels were taken for the king. The gross income of the priory at its dissolution was estimated at over £1572 making it one of the twenty most wealthy monasteries in England.

Then, perhaps suspecting the monks of fraud, or of hiding further treasure, they ordered the coffin of St Cuthbert, high on its pedestal behind the high altar, to be broken open. An account written later in the sixteenth century describes what the goldsmith, who broke the inner coffin is supposed to have found: 'the body lying whole, uncorrupt, with his face bare, and his beard as it had been a fortnight's growth and all his vestments upon him, as he was accustomed to say Mass withal'.

Dr Henley, standing below, ordered the smith to throw the bones down. The man replied that he could not, because they were still held together by sinews and skin. There was nothing for it but that Dr Henley and Dr Leigh must themselves climb up to see.

Later, when the famous shrine had been destroyed, the body of St Cuthbert was buried on the same spot, in a simple tomb which lies there today.

No serious scandal was reported among the Durham monks but the priory was to be 'dissolved' like all the others. On 31 December 1539 Prior Whitehead handed over the priory to the king's officials. He was left in charge for the time being but in May 1541 a new constitution was issued. Prior White- head became dean of the cathedral and twelve monks were made 'prebendaries'. The others were scattered about the diocese as parish priests but the great cathedral of Durham was to survive, as it still does, under the rule of a Dean and Chapter of Anglican clergy.

Durham was more fortunate than many other monasteries which were quickly plundered for the valuable building material and so fell into ruin. Because this priory was so much a part of the great cathedral, the buildings were not destroyed. Many books were left in the library and lands belonging to the priory were transferred to the dean and prebendaries to provide income for the cathedral.

But the beauty and dignity of the monastic ceremonies came to an end. Many beautiful things, the work of artists and craftsmen over the centuries, were done away with. Dean William Wittingham had all the carvings and brasses destroyed in the 1570s. His wife burned the famous banner of St Cuthbert,

used the stone holy water bowl as a sink in her kitchen and is said to have set tombstones from the monks' cemetery as paving stones in her house in the town.

Although the church services continued and a choir school was set up again in the 1550s the grandeur of earlier days was gone. Crowds of pilgrims no longer crossed the Wear and climbed the rocky heights to visit the shrine of the saint of the north. Today, however, the pilgrims are replaced by the thousands of visitors who come to see the cathedral: the achievement of the monks lives on and they will never be completely forgotten.

Today the tomb of St Cuthbert is marked by a simple stone slab in the floor behind the high altar.